Original title:
The Green Haven

Copyright © 2025 Creative Arts Management OÜ
All rights reserved.

Author: Elias Montgomery
ISBN HARDBACK: 978-1-80581-770-3
ISBN PAPERBACK: 978-1-80581-297-5
ISBN EBOOK: 978-1-80581-770-3

Whispers of Verdant Dreams

In the forest where squirrels prance,
The frogs sing in a silly dance.
Mice wear hats, the rabbits giggle,
Nature's jokes make the trees wiggle.

Sunlight tickles the grass so bright,
While butterflies flirt in sheer delight.
A turtle wearing shades of green,
Claims he's the fastest, but where's the scene?

Sanctuary of Swaying Leaves

The branches sway with joyful cheer,
As secret whispers fill the ear.
A raccoon shimmies, what a sight!
His dance ends with a comical bite.

Chirping birds crack silly jokes,
While ants march in their tiny cloaks.
Moss spreads laughter on the ground,
As gnomes begin their jolly round.

Emerald Embrace

In fields of green, the sheep put on
A wooly show as the sun is gone.
They huddle close, share tales of fame,
While one insists it's all a game.

The grasshoppers leap, thinking they're stars,
Kicking it back with jokes from Mars.
A dandelion whispers soft and low,
That tickling toupees make the best show.

A Tapestry of Nature's Solace

Buttercups giggle, painting the ground,
As daisies twirl, swirling all around.
The sun says hi with a wink and glare,
While a bear tries yoga with comical flair.

Pine cones gossip, it's quite absurd,
While willows murmur a secret word.
Together they laugh in vibrant tunes,
In this haven under merry moons.

The Lure of the Landscape

In a meadow wide and bright,
Where daisies dance with delight,
A rabbit wears a jaunty hat,
And winks at every passing cat.

The trees play tag, they twist and shout,
While squirrels scribble tales about,
A butterfly with dreams of flight,
Swaps gossip with a bird mid-flight.

Chasing Sunbeams

The sun spills laughter on the grass,
As kiddos run, no time to pass.
They slip on slides of golden rays,
And giggle through the sunny maze.

Their shadows mimic all they do,
A dance of silliness in view.
They chase a wink from clouds so high,
While ants parade beneath the sky.

Green Shadows at Twilight

As evening wraps its cozy cloak,
The trees tell tales; they love to poke.
A raccoon sneezes, starts a fit,
While fireflies giggle in a bit.

The moon joins in with a playful grin,
As crickets start their buzzing din.
A fox wears shoes that are too tight,
And twirls around in pure delight.

Echoes of Evergreen

In whispers soft, the pines confess,
They plot a scheme, a tiny mess.
A porcupine plays peek-a-boo,
With a hedgehog that's skewed askew.

The ferns gossip with the stones,
While owls wear crowns made of bones.
Each branch a jest, each leaf a joke,
Nature's laughter, gently spoke.

Nestled Among the Trees

In a spot where leaves play peek-a-boo,
Squirrels parade in acorn hats, it's true!
The birds gossip, all chirp and chatter,
While rabbits hop like they're on a platter.

A raccoon stands guard, it's quite absurd,
With binoculars made from a tiny bird.
He's the self-appointed watchman today,
As cats scowl and plot their ambush play.

A Garden of Serendipity

In my patch, the tomatoes are wearing shades,
While cucumbers dance in their leafy glades.
Gnomes breakdance on the garden floor,
   While lazy bees snooze and snore!

Sunflowers flirt with the bumblebees,
While carrots gossip in the cool, soft breeze.
The radishes swoon, blushing quite red,
Dreaming of winning the veggie bread.

Sweetness in the Swaying Grass

In fields where the daisies throw a party,
The butterflies dance, not one looks tardy.
Grasshoppers joke, and they leap with flair,
While ants form a band in a grand affair.

Picnics gather, oh what a sight!
Sandwiches giggle with pure delight.
Lemonade teases with bubbles and cheer,
As ants march in, singing loud and clear.

Treetop Reverie

Up in the branches where the silliness thrives,
Monkeys throw fruit like it's their high-fives.
Parrots crack jokes, their humor so fine,
While sloths swing slowly, just sipping their wine.

A raccoon takes photos, his lens all askew,
Capuchins fashion a wild rendezvous.
Every critter smiles, in nature's embrace,
As laughter and joy scatter all over the place.

Ferns and Forgotten Paths

In shadows deep, the ferns do sway,
Like dancers lost, they play all day.
With mossy hats and roots that cling,
They gossip softly about the spring.

A squirrel sneaks in, his acorn prize,
He trips on roots, oh what a rise!
The ferns all laugh, they wiggle wide,
As the squirrel blushes—what a ride!

Old paths are tangled, a maze so fun,
You'll lose your way, or just run!
With giggles echoing off the trees,
Who knew a walk could bring such Glee?

Yet every turn bears silly sights,
A frog in boots that surely blights.
So lace your shoes and join the spree,
In this green giggle, wild and free!

In Bloom's Gentle Grasp

Petals laugh as the bees do hum,
They dance a jig, oh what a scrum!
In hues so bright, they tease the air,
A floral showdown, who'll get the flair?

Butterflies waltz without a care,
While daisies dodge their fluffy snare.
"Oh please, stop stepping on my toes!"
Cried tulip to a rose, as petals close.

A bumblebee dons a tiny vest,
In search of pollen, he is the best!
With every flop, he can't quite steer,
The blooms all laugh, "What brings you here?"

Yet in this chaos, joy abounds,
With every giggle in leafy grounds.
For life is better with color and cheer,
In jest and bloom, we draw near!

Canopies of Calm

Beneath the trees, where whispers cling,
A parrot squawks, "Hey, look at me sing!"
With branches wide stretching to the sky,
All creatures watch the antics fly by.

A chipmunk juggles nuts with glee,
"Come one, come all, be amazed at me!"
But as he tumbles, in quite a flap,
He lands in moss, with a thudding slap.

Sunlight drips through the leafy maze,
Casting funny shadows that twist and graze.
A cat naps soundly with dreams of fish,
While tangled roots weave a final wish.

"Is that the sound of popcorn popping?"
Sounds of laughter, oh, they're swapping!
In every nook, joy finds a place,
In this calm canopy, all can embrace!

The Dance of Sunlight and Shade

Sunlight twirls in a golden dress,
While shade replies, "Don't you mess!"
They spin around in a dizzy art,
Tickling leaves with a playful heart.

A rabbit hops between the beams,
Chasing light as if it seems.
"Oh wait!" he yells, "Did I just trip?"
In shadows, he gives a little flip!

The grass whispers secrets, so sly and sweet,
While sunlight bursts in—a joyous greet.
"Have you tried to catch a dancing ray?"
Shade chuckles back, "Well, it's my play!"

Together they whirl, a puzzling scheme,
Inviting laughter, igniting a dream.
In the warmth of light, let humor spark,
In jests of green, we leave our mark!

Dappled Light

In a forest of mismatched socks,
Sunshine dances on playful rocks.
Trees giggle as the breeze runs through,
Winking at rabbits who don't have a clue.

Squirrels hold acorn races at noon,
While birds serenade to a comical tune.
A toad performs, slick and spry,
His warty dance a delight to the eye.

Frogs in tuxedos sing out loud,
Thinking they're part of a fancy crowd.
The shadows tease, they twist and twirl,
As nature's humor begins to unfurl.

Soft Sound

Rustling leaves whisper jokes on the way,
Each cackle of critters brightens the day.
Bubbles of laughter float in the air,
Even the trees chuckle without a care.

Crickets cracking puns by the pond,
A platypus nods to a snail's beyond.
Hares hopping wildly, kick up the muck,
While building a castle just for pure luck.

Echoes of mirth bounce off the ground,
As butterflies flutter and giggles abound.
Caterpillars share jests in their haste,
In this soft sound, no sadness is placed.

Canopy of Calm

Under the arch of a goofy tree,
Laughter whispers, wild and free.
Branches bow with a comical grin,
Shaking loose the giggles within.

Gnomes knit stories on wobbly chairs,
While shadows giggle without any cares.
The couch of moss hugs in delight,
Inviting all for a soft, silly night.

In this calm space, where silliness flows,
The wind tells tales that everyone knows.
It teases the leaves, makes them sway,
Crafting a home for merry play.

Laughter Among the Lilies

Blooming flowers don bright, silly hats,
In a garden where laughter is where it's at.
Bees wear suspenders, buzzing in rhyme,
Tickling the tulips just for a good time.

Daffodils snicker at the daisies' plight,
Trying to dance but only in flight.
The lavender twins play hide and seek,
While crickets crack jokes, almost mystique.

Each petal's a laugh, a twinkle, a cheer,
In this haven of giggles, all creatures appear.
Amidst all the joy, they bloom without strife,
In this riotous garden, laughter is life.

Sanctuary of the Senses

Sniffing the air brings a whiff of fun,
Sweet scents of laughter warm like the sun.
Tickling fragrances dance on the breeze,
While plump berries gossip among the trees.

Hummingbirds flap with a zing and a zap,
While a sleeping bear wears a curious cap.
A whiff of mischief swirls in the space,
As frogs hold a revelry, just to embrace.

Colors explode in a riotous show,
Each shade giggles as it starts to glow.
This sanctuary thrives on whimsy and cheer,
With senses attuned to magic drawing near.

Secrets in the Thicket

In the woods where squirrels play,
Nuts are hidden away each day.
A raccoon dons a masquerade,
In the thicket, secrets invade.

Deer gossip under the stars,
Whispering tales of candy bars.
A frog croaks like a diva,
While bugs twirl in a grand fiesta.

Bunnies hop with a cheeky grin,
Dancing like they're all swimmin'.
Every rustle, a giggle found,
In this thicket, pure joy abounds.

Blossoms of Tranquility

The flowers giggle in the breeze,
Tickled gently by buzzing bees.
The tulips argue on who's best,
While daisies join the silly jest.

With petals bright and smiles wide,
Lilies wear their hats with pride.
A sunflower claims it's the king,
As butterflies form a merry ring.

Petunias tell a cackle joke,
In the garden, laughter's soaked.
Among the blooms, all is bright,
Humor blooms in morning's light.

Meadow's Embrace

In meadows wide, the sheep conspire,
To form a band and sing desire.
They bleat a tune, off-key and bold,
As daisies blush from tales retold.

A cricket brings his finest hat,
Hoping to charm a flirty cat.
While butterflies dance with finesse,
Creating chaos, more or less.

The grass tickles feet, don't you see?
As pranks unfold with glee and glee.
In this embrace, laughter reigns,
With each soft breeze, joy never wanes.

The Hidden Grove

In a grove where shadows play,
Mice throw shadows, that's their way.
A lizard claims he's been a star,
While crickets chirp from near and far.

Batteries for buzzers? Who needs these?
When all around is laughter and ease.
The trees wear spectacles, it's a sight,
Keeping a watch, both day and night.

Squirrels hold a council, tight-knit,
Debating over who's more fit.
A robin dances, hops about,
In the grove, there's never doubt.

Garden of Tranquil Murmurs

In a garden where squirrels dance,
Flowers giggle as they prance.
Bees wear hats and laugh with glee,
While butterflies sip tea with a plea.

A snail's slow stroll turns into a race,
Worms throw parties in mud's embrace.
With daisies whispering secrets bright,
It's a silly sight, oh what a delight!

The sun tickles leaves, making them shake,
Garden gnomes trip, oh what a mistake!
A breeze hums tunes of playful cheer,
While ladybugs dance without any fear.

In this whimsical patch of nature's fun,
Laughter echoes, the day is won.
So come join the jest, don't be shy,
In this garden, laughter floats high.

Beneath Canopies of Hope

Beneath trees where shadows play,
A raccoon wears shades, having a day.
Chipmunks hold a talent show,
With acorns tossed like confetti low.

Squirrels play hopscotch on a log,
While a frog croaks like a silly fog.
The leaves rustle with giggles bright,
As crickets sing songs into the night.

A wise old owl misreads the clock,
Countless straws yet no one shocked.
With every tick, each tickling time,
All laugh along, their joy in rhyme.

So under this dome of nature's weird,
Come share in laughter, forget your fears.
Let whimsy reign as we cheer and sway,
For joy's the game we love to play!

Lush Refuge of the Heart

In a haven where felines plot,
Cats wear crowns, who knew they'd thought?
A dog tries yoga near the stream,
Barking zen while chasing a dream.

Tilted mushrooms offer shade,
While toadstools in circles, a parade.
All critters gather for the fun,
And the sun grins, its race not run.

Fragrant blooms boast of silly scents,
The flowers argue, it's quite intense.
Buzzing bees, the judges with flair,
Seek the finest bloom from their airborne chair.

So gather 'round, both old and new,
In this refuge where laughter grew.
A place for heart and humor to blend,
Where joy's just a moment away my friend!

Mosaic of Moss and Light

A tapestry of colors made in jest,
Mossy carpets offer a comfy nest.
Frogs in bow ties croak in style,
While lizards slide by with a cheeky smile.

A clever fox plays hide and seek,
With drapes of ferns, a playful sneak.
Their giggles echo through the trees,
As beetles race down the mossy breeze.

Sunlight sprinkles like confetti bright,
On quirky plants that sway with delight.
The whimsical whispers of the plants,
Comfy and quirky, everyone prances.

In this patchwork where smiles abound,
Nature's blend spins laughter round.
So take a seat, let giggles take flight,
In this lovely mosaic of joy and light.

Secrets Beneath the Foliage

Underneath the leafy roof,
A squirrel's got his secret hoot.
He's hiding nuts for winter's bluff,
But can't resist some acorn fluff.

The grass has eyes, it winks in glee,
Dancing shadows tease the bee.
The flowers giggle in the breeze,
Telling tales of secret keys.

A rabbit wears a tiny hat,
Declares himself the king of chat!
The ants march on with tiny drums,
In a parade of bumbling sums.

So peek beneath the emerald cloak,
Where life unfolds with every joke.
Nature whispers, laughs, and plays,
In the leafy, merry maze.

The Breath of the Earth

The trees all share a giggly sigh,
As birds exchange their silly why.
A worm crawls by and stops to brag,
About the size of his last snag.

A breeze tickles the daisies' face,
Who toss their heads in a funny race.
The shadows chase the sunlight beams,
And plants conspire to steal dreams.

The soil's deep laughter bubbles up,
As raindrops join the dancing cup.
The puddles splash with joyful shrieks,
While frogs reveal their comic peaks.

So breathe in deep, feel nature's fun,
Where every leaf has just begun.
In this joyful, witty spree,
Earth laughs out loud, come join with me!

Harmonies of the Leafy Realm

In a symphony of chirps and croaks,
The trees add rhythm to the jokes.
Frogs play tunes from lily pads,
While insects buzz with giddy fads.

The branches sway, a conga line,
Leaves twirl and twist, it's all divine.
Each rustle comes with a hearty cheer,
As woodland critters gather near.

A gopher dons a funky tie,
His digging makes the daisies fly.
The sunbeams bounce like playful sprites,
In this leafy dance of wild delights.

So join the choir beneath the sun,
Where every note means nature's fun.
In this melody of green so bright,
Each laugh resounds, a pure delight!

Sylvan Respite

In the woods where laughter blooms,
A fox spins tales from old costumes.
Beneath the boughs, the humor flows,
With every rustle, merriment grows.

The mushrooms wear their fancy hats,
While critters gossip like old mats.
A hedgehog serves some tea and cake,
With tiny spoons for giggles' sake.

The breezes join the happy chat,
As woodland critters dance and spat.
Acorns roll with giggling glee,
As nature's party spills into spree.

So take a seat on mossy ground,
Where joy and laughter can be found.
In this sylvan space, unwind,
With every corner, fun's designed!

Beauty Between the Branches

In a tree where squirrels chatter,
A raccoon tried to climb a ladder.
He slipped, he fell, his pride laid bare,
Now he just hangs out with the pear.

The birds conspire with cheeky tweets,
Playing hide and seek, oh what feats!
They challenge passersby to dance,
While leaves swirl around in a trance.

Beneath the boughs, an old tortoise,
Wears flower crowns; oh what a bonus!
He sways to music only he hears,
Chasing dreams, conquering fears.

At sunset, shadows start to prance,
The insects gather, join the dance.
In this woods, nothing's too strange,
Every creature loves to exchange.

Still Waters Run Green

In a pond where frogs do croak,
One wore glasses, fancied a joke.
He pondered hard on what to say,
Then slipped on lily pads—oh, hooray!

Goldfish gossip, float with flair,
Dancing bubbles fill the air.
One said, "Is it just me who sees,
That minnows can wear tiny tees?"

The dragonflies sport hats so tall,
They host tea parties, with a ball.
The reeds lean in to share their tales,
Of fishy friends and mischievous gales.

As twilight wraps the world in dreams,
The water glows with moonlit beams.
And all agree, with chuckles bright,
That laughter echoes through the night.

Pathways of Peace

On a path where daisies sway,
A rabbit danced, without delay.
He tripped on roots and rolled in grass,
Chasing his friend, a snail with sass.

Gnomes all gathered, held their hats,
To share tales of curious chats.
They laughed at how a toad could sing,
While wearing shoes meant for a king.

Beneath tall trees, the shadows play,
With all the bunnies on parade.
They leap and hop without a care,
As butterflies float, everywhere.

In this realm where giggles bloom,
Every corner banishes gloom.
So join the jest, let spirits soar,
In nature's smile, there's always more!

Harvest of Hope

Amidst the crops, a scarecrow grins,
He boasts about his wins and spins.
With crows as friends, they share the pie,
Together, they reach for the sky.

Pumpkins roll in a game of chase,
While corn stalks join in the race.
A hedgehog dreams of fancy hats,
While finding snacks from cheeky rats.

The sun brings joy, the rain brings cheer,
As critters gather from far and near.
In fields of laughter, hope grows bright,
With every turn, there's pure delight.

So join the feast, or take a stroll,
Let laughter fill your heart and soul.
For in this place where smiles are sown,
You'll find a joy that's all your own.

Splendor in Growth

In a patch that glows so bright,
Plants wear green robes, what a sight!
Twirling leaves in a dance so spry,
Even the weeds seem to comply!

Bugs in hats, and ants in line,
Sipping nectar, oh so fine!
Garden gnomes with silly grins,
Plotting where the fun begins!

Sunflowers gossip, tall and proud,
While daisies form a giggling crowd.
Nature laughs, it's quite a show,
As rabbits hop to steal the glow!

So embrace this world of silliness,
Where growth and joy find their finesse.
In this garden, a comical home,
Every plant's a friend, never alone.

A Haven of Hues

Colors splash in every place,
Nature's palette, a lively race.
Tulips red and violets blue,
Whisper secrets in the dew.

Frogs wear ties, they leap with flair,
Bees have stories to share with air.
Petunias chuckle, bright and bold,
While the marigolds boast tales untold!

Clouds roll in, a playful tease,
Guessing when they'll rain on these.
Sunshine winked, a bright reprieve,
Nature's circus, oh, we believe!

In this realm of vibrant play,
Each hue stands out in a quirky way.
Let laughter bloom under the sun,
In a haven where colors have fun.

Glistening Dewdrops

Morning breaks with tiny pearls,
On leaf tips, they dance and twirl.
Each drop a giggle, shining bright,
Making grass blades sparkle with delight.

A ladybug slips, then trips on dew,
Laughing friends, they cheer anew.
"Don't worry, friend, it's just a slide!"
They roll and tumble, side by side!

Reflections play on petals soft,
Where butterflies drift, aloft.
Dewdrops wink, they know their game,
Nature's pranksters, wild and tame!

Glistening treasures at dawn's embrace,
Fill the world with cheer and grace.
Join the laughter, stake your claim,
In the garden's joyful frame.

Enfolded in Nature

Wrapped in green, oh what a sight,
Trees wear coats of pure delight.
Squirrels chatter, plotting snacks,
While pigeons strut, in fancy tracks.

A rabbit pops out, doing tricks,
Juggling acorns with some kicks.
Each plant plays its funny role,
In this bash, they're on a stroll!

Sunlight pours like syrup sweet,
Tickling trees and tickling feet.
Nature hums a silly tune,
As shadows dance, beneath the moon.

So come and join this comical fest,
With laughter sprouting, it's the best!
In every leaf, a joke to find,
For nature's fun is intertwined!

Flora's Gentle Lullaby

In a garden of laughter, flowers giggle,
Bees wear tiny hats, dance, wiggle,
The daisies chat, plotting a prank,
While roses spill tea in their floral bank.

A sunflower sings off-key, what a scene,
Tomato plants gossip, all in between,
The lilacs laugh, they can't hold it in,
As vines tie shoes at the garden's chin.

Butterflies wear socks, who would have known?
While worms slide down slides made of stone,
Thyme tells tales under humor's spell,
In this playful patch, all is well!

At dusk, the moon joins, a cheeky light,
As crickets refrain, taking flight,
In Flora's arms, dreams find their way,
In laughter's embrace, they giggle and sway.

Haven of Harmony

In a nook where the daisies throw wild tea parties,
Sipping sunlight and wearing bright charties,
All the weeds tell jokes from times of yore,
While ladybugs roll, begging for more!

The trees clap their leaves, what a sound!
While the peacocks strut, spinning 'round and 'round,
Frogs wear bow ties, all dignified,
As the ants pull a wagon on their little ride.

The clouds send hiccups down from the sky,
While the sun chuckles, not wanting to cry,
In this cheery space, laughter entwines,
Nature's own show, on laughter it dines!

At the day's curtain call, stars lend their smiles,
Giggling crickets play on through the miles,
In this joyful haven, all feel at ease,
Where giggles of nature float softly on the breeze.

Petals and Promises

Petals pirouette on a soft spring breeze,
While hedgehogs tell tales of slick little bees,
Snails wear their shells like new, wild hats,
While laughing potholders serve out snacks!

The tulips tumble like clowns in a row,
With giggles and whispers, they steal the show,
A surprise confetti of pollen delight,
As the daisies tumble, oh what a sight!

Butterflies, in stilts, decide to parade,
As silly raindrops hop, unafraid,
In a rhythm of petals, they dance and sway,
Here, every moment, a frollicking play!

As the stars glimmer in applause from above,
The flowers share secrets of friendship and love,
Nestled in cozy under the moon's glow,
Promises linger; here, joy is the flow.

Rooted in Stillness

In the shade of the trees, where laughter abounds,
Roots twist and turn, in whimsical rounds,
Bugs hold a summit to settle old scores,
As mushrooms wear jackets, discussing outdoors.

A wise old oak tells riddles so witty,
As the shrubs crack jokes, oh aren't they gritty?
The deer in their mocktail hats sip away,
While squirrels toss acorns in a funny ballet!

The wind whispers secrets, tickles the grass,
While cinematographic moments will pass,
Nature's own chuckles float high in the air,
With each playful breeze weaving joy everywhere!

In this zone of calm, every root can joke,
Where even the moss is known to poke,
With a giggle or two, all is still fun,
As laughter and silence fuse into one.

Lost in the Lush

In a forest where squirrels play,
I lost my way, oh what a day!
The trees, they whispered silly tunes,
While birds donned hats and roasted prunes.

A hedgehog winked and asked for fries,
A moose wore shades, oh what a surprise!
I tripped on roots, oh what a tease,
The ferns just giggled in the breeze.

The mushrooms danced a little jig,
The owls debated, who's really big?
I laughed so hard I nearly cried,
In this wild place where joy can't hide.

Then a rabbit offered me a drink,
It tasted green, made me rethink.
With all this fun, I'd surely stay,
But who knew nature could be so gay!

Flourish of the Fields

In fields so bright that tickle the eye,
Bumblebees buzz with a cheeky sigh.
The daisies gossip in hues so bold,
While a sunflower stands to break the mold.

A chicken clucks, wearing a crown,
Strutting around like it owns the town.
She pecks at grains and rolls in dirt,
Quirky antics, oh how they flirt!

Then comes a pig with a muddy snort,
He slips and slides, quite a sport!
Crickets play tunes on blades so green,
The happiest bugs you've ever seen.

Laughter echoes through meadow and glen,
With silliness bursting from each little den!
We pick wildflowers, toss them in air,
In this field, joy is found everywhere!

Whispered Wishes in the Wind

The breeze told secrets, old and new,
Of kites that fly and clouds that skew.
A duck quacked jokes, with a wink so sly,
While butterflies twirled, oh how they fly!

I wished for snacks and a sunny treat,
But found a snail with fast-moving feet.
He grinned and said, 'You're way too slow!'
In this realm, even slowpokes steal the show.

The grass tickled my toes with zest,
While ladybugs fought for the best nest.
They bickered and squabbled, all in jest,
Nature's comedy is truly the best!

So, we laughed with leaves, swayed with the breeze,
In shared harmony, oh what a tease!
Whispered wishes danced in the air,
In this funny place, joy everywhere!

Nectar of Life

In a garden where nectar flows like dreams,
Bees buzz around with silly schemes.
A ladybug played a game of tag,
While a butterfly tried to brag and brag.

A flower sneezed, oh what a sight!
It fluffed its petals, too silly to fight.
The tulip laughed, gave a gentle sigh,
'Bless you!' it said, as it waved goodbye.

Nearby, a worm wrote poems in dirt,
With lines so witty, you'd never get hurt.
They tickled the roots and made them giggle,
In this garden dance, life would jiggle.

As dusk settled down, the stars peeped through,
The bugs had a party, just for a few.
In the laughter of night, life took a dive,
In this wild place, we all felt alive!

Verdant Dreams

In a field where grass grows tall,
Silly bugs have a grand ball.
They dance on leaves, with so much flair,
Who knew they'd have a party there?

Bumblebees wear tiny hats,
While crickets sit like chubby cats.
The daisies giggle, swaying proud,
Welcoming the grasshopper crowd.

A toad croaks jokes, oh what a riot,
While butterflies flutter, they can't keep quiet.
The sun peeks in, the frogs must hide,
In this zany lawn, there's nowhere to bide.

As twilight falls, the fireflies gleam,
Nobody wants to end this dream.
They twirl and whirl in moonlight's grace,
In this wacky green, they find their place.

The Enchanted Glade

In a glade where squirrels play chess,
Raccoons in capes claim they're the best.
Trees wear hats made of fine moss,
Arguing 'til they nearly toss!

Mice with ties boast of their cheese,
While rabbits tease, "We move with ease!"
The sun, a jester, casts quirky light,
On this stage where all is bright.

Dancing ferns whisper funny tales,
Even the daisies laugh and wail.
A hedgehog rolls in, humor intact,
Dropping quips that are quite abstract.

As the moon rises, the jokes find flight,
The forest fills with laughter, a joyous night.
Here in the glade, no one is moody,
Just a band of friends and absolute goofiness!

Fragments of the Forest

Among branches, a parrot sings,
Mocking the owls with crazy flings.
A deer trips on roots, oh so sly,
Blushing beneath the bright blue sky.

The woodpecker's rhythm makes you dance,
While mischievous mice take a chance.
They throw acorns, giggling with glee,
"Catch us if you can," they chant with plea!

In this patch where the wild things play,
Every leaf hides a new display.
The berries wink, inviting a taste,
While the critters plan their wild little haste.

As day fades away, the giggles rejoice,
The whispers surround like a vibrant voice.
In fragmented laughter, the forest resides,
Where every creature, in silliness, abides.

Sanctuary Beneath the Canopy

Under the shade where shadows dwell,
Frogs tell stories, oh do tell!
A turtle critiques their latest prank,
"I'm too old for this," he said with a crank.

Squirrels dangle, tails in a twist,
While chipmunks argue, "Did you miss?"
Acorns fly in a comical duel,
While a wise old owl observes, "Oh, you fools!"

In this haven with branches high,
Laughter echoes, as squirrels fly.
Mushrooms giggle, tickling the ground,
In this sanctuary, joy can be found.

As crickets chirp their nightly tune,
The forest chuckles beneath the moon.
Here every creature knows such delight,
In the canopy, life is a funny sight!

An Oasis of Life

In the garden, gnomes are fun,
They drink their drinks and run,
Bouncing to the beat of bees,
Dancing with the swaying trees.

Sunshine slips through leafy greens,
Where squirrels wear their tiny jeans,
The flowers gossip, oh so loud,
While ants parade, oh so proud.

A frog sings tunes for all to hear,
While turtles chuckle, full of cheer,
With laughter sprouting all around,
In this arena, joy is found.

So grab a hat and join the fun,
The antics here have just begun,
In nature's playground, wild and bright,
Every leaf's a comic sight.

Serene Echoes of the Woods

In the woods where shadows play,
A moose attempts to dance ballet,
While raccoons sing in harmony,
As owls sip tea with no-one but me.

The trees exchange their silly jokes,
While chipmunks giggle at the folks,
Frogs leap in their finest attire,
While squirrels hold a dance-off choir.

A deer wears glasses far too big,
He sips some juice, does a little jig,
And nearby, a hedgehog with flair,
Strikes poses like a runway bear.

Here in whispers of the woods,
Life's just one big laugh-filled mood,
Nature's antics spin around,
In this joyful, playful ground.

Shadows of Whispering Pines

Underneath the tall pine trees,
A goat swings by, enjoying cheese,
And raccoons in tuxedos prance,
While squirrels all join the dance.

The shadows play peek-a-boo with light,
A bear in shades shouts, 'What a sight!'
The chipmunks toss their acorn hats,
As owls debate the silliest stats.

With every gust, the pines will creak,
They gossip tales of the week,
A breeze carries laughter through the air,
With echoes of joy, it's everywhere.

In this scene of warmth and glee,
Where every critter's wild and free,
Shadows dance in merry lines,
Oh, how fun is life among pines!

Emerald Enclave

In this spot where laughter blooms,
The flowers play their silly tunes,
A snail races with a tortoise slow,
While bees in hats steal quite the show.

The grass has whispers, full of wit,
As rabbits dance, never quit,
While butterflies wear neon brights,
They twirl and spin on sunny heights.

A hedgehog hosts a trivia night,
With all his pals, what a delight!
They argue on who knows the best,
In this enclave, it's quite a jest.

So come join in, leave all your woes,
Where laughter grows beneath the bows,
In this realm of color and cheer,
Every moment's a memory here.

Dance of the Wild Ferns

In the forest, ferns do sway,
Twisting, turning, in a play.
They wave their fronds with such delight,
Who knew plants could dance all night?

Bumblebees join in with glee,
They buzz along, as if to plea.
"Let's throw a party, join the fun!"
Who knew nature's ball had begun?

Sunlight sparkles on the dew,
While critters groove, a lively crew.
A squirrel twirls, a rabbit hops,
In this green realm, the fun never stops.

In every leaf, a laugh can bloom,
With a sprinkle of joy, here's the room.
Join the ferns, just take a chance,
In this dance, you can prance!

Secrets of the Soil

Underneath, where secrets grow,
Wiggly worms put on a show.
They wiggle this and twist and that,
"Dear grass, your roots are looking flat!"

Hidden treasures in the dirt,
A lost old shoe, a piece of shirt.
The ants convene with tiny grins,
Plotting how they'll steal your bins!

Moles are digging, causing fuss,
While toads sit back and ride the bus.
"Mud bath time!" they croak with cheer,
This soil party's the highlight of the year.

So if you think it's just old earth,
Remember it's a place of mirth.
A universe beneath our feet,
Where every creature has a beat!

Serenity in the Shade

Beneath the trees, a cool retreat,
Lazily, the critters meet.
Squirrels nap on branches high,
While lazy clouds drift in the sky.

A rabbit snores, a turtle sighs,
In this haven, where time flies.
Chirping birds share silly tales,
Of lost acorns and runaway snails.

Umbrellas of leaves, a green delight,
Throwing shadows, dancing light.
Here, no rush—just take a seat,
The breeze provides a comfy beat.

So here's to shade where laughter rings,
And every critter has its flings.
Whispers of joy in every rustle,
Nature's own cozy huddle.

A Mosaic of Wilderness

Colors splatter across the ground,
The wild's palette, swirling around.
Berries laugh in shades of red,
While flowers boast of what they said.

A butterfly flits, "Catch me if you can!"
While frogs make bets on who's the man.
A raccoon sneaks, as mischief brews,
In this wild space, there's no lost shoes!

The brook gurgles in a giggly spree,
Mimicking the joy of a lively bee.
Each critter adds to the carnival,
In this wilderness, it's a free-for-all!

Nature's canvas, bright and bold,
With stories of laughter, yet untold.
So join the fun, don't be a bore,
In this wilderness, you'll find much more!

Solitude in the Thicket

In the thicket where I roam,
Even bushes seem like home.
A squirrel mocks with a little dance,
While I trip over roots in a trance.

Leaves gossip like old friends,
Telling tales that never end.
A caterpillar gives me a wink,
As I sit and sip my drink.

Birds chirp jokes from tree to tree,
Flying high, too fast for me.
I chuckle as I lose my shoe,
Nature's laugh is bright and true.

So here I stay, a hidden gem,
Amongst the ferns, a real mayhem.
In solitude, I find pure glee,
With only giggles from a bumblebee.

Verdant Verses

In a leaf crown, I reign supreme,
With grasshoppers plotting my dream.
Frogs croak puns from the nearby bog,
While I'm stuck, a giggling hog.

The daisies spin in reckless glee,
Daring me to join their spree.
I trip over roots, but who can care?
Nature's laughter fills the air.

Mice throw shade as they scurry past,
Pointing out my fashion faux pas at last.
But I laugh, sporting my leafy hat,
With dandelions stuck, how about that?

In this jungle of color and sound,
I lose my worries, never found.
With a giggle shared by all around,
In verdant cheer, my joy is crowned.

Cradled by Nature's Warmth

Nestled in moss, I start to dream,
The sun glimmers, a golden beam.
Bees fetch tea in tiny cups,
As I lounge, just needing some ups.

A chipmunk acts like a fancy host,
Fluffing his cheeks, he boasts the most.
I chuckle as I nod along,
While nature hums its silly song.

The flowers gossip, their petals bright,
Sharing notes on who's in sight.
I wave at a butterfly looking grand,
But trip over a pebble, oh dear, I'm bland!

Cradled softly in this embrace,
Each giggle blooms in every space.
I'd rather be here than anywhere,
With laughing buds, and fresh spring air.

Pathways to Tranquility

Wandering paths where the wild things play,
I lose my way, go astray.
A rabbit teases as I chase,
Through bushes wide, in a silly race.

The sun peeks through, a wink or jest,
While I stumble, full of zest.
A signpost points to nowhere nice,
But that's okay, I'll roll the dice.

Laughter bubbles from brooks nearby,
As frogs leap high, oh me, oh my!
I clap my hands, then trip again,
In this park of giggles, I'll never complain.

Paths unfurl with nature's charm,
Where every slip leads to a balm.
I dance with trees, and oh, what fun!
In joyful steps, we've only begun!

The Lure of Hidden Groves

In the woods where squirrels prance,
A dance-off with a flower's stance.
Chipmunks chatter, plotting schemes,
While mushrooms giggle, or so it seems.

With each step, you might just scare,
A tree frog jumping from its lair.
The sunbeams play a game of tag,
Where even the shadows start to brag.

Bumblebees wear tiny crowns,
While daisies sport their floppy gowns.
In this grove, it's all a jest,
The bark's a comedian at its best.

So wander forth, if you're quite brave,
With nature's laughter, you shall save.
A chuckle here, a chuckle there,
In hidden woods, there's joy to spare.

Echoes of the Leafy Lullaby

In leafy beds, the shadows play,
While owls debate the time of day.
The wind whispers secrets in the trees,
"Who tickled me?" the branches tease.

A raccoon in mischief wears a hat,
While ants strategize, 'Where's the cat?'
Chirping crickets hold a choir,
With rhymes that set their hearts on fire.

The mushrooms host a midnight feast,
Where playful sprites munch on yeast.
With every giggle, trees sway low,
In this silly world of ebb and flow.

So join the chorus, don't be shy,
Laugh with the flowers as you fly.
In the rhythm of the ancient song,
Nature's humor is never wrong.

The Symphony of Flora

Bees are buzzing in a band,
While daisies drift like grains of sand.
The violets hum a tune so sweet,
As the roots tap dance beneath your feet.

Swaying branches clap their hands,
As laughter echoes through the lands.
Each leaf participates in this play,
With silly gestures, come what may.

The ferns yet whisper, oh so low,
While mushrooms shout, "Hey, look at me go!"
A symphony of giggles fills the air,
In this concert of flora, none a care.

So take your seat upon the ground,
And let nature's silliness abound.
With every note and every sound,
In the woodland's laughter, joy is found.

Timeless Tales of the Woodland

Once a tree could spin a yarn,
About the day it met a barn.
A squirrel climbed to share its tale,
While hedgehogs laughed and shook their quail.

The babbling brook, an old, wise sage,
Claims it's seen queens in a rage.
With a wink it spills the tea,
Of the leaves' last raucous spree.

Mice sit round with ears so keen,
For jokes by the great, green unseen.
The acorns giggle, "What's next?" "Who knows!"
In this woodland, laughter always flows.

So gather 'round, come hear their glee,
In timeless tales of absurdity.
For every tree has stories spun,
Where even the sun can have some fun.

Nature's Embrace

In a field of daisies wide,
Bumblebees take a joyride.
Frogs wear crowns, they leap and croak,
One tried to catch a drifting boat!

Squirrels dance with acorn hats,
Chasing tails and all of that.
A snail took part in a race,
But left the crowd with a slow pace!

Dancing leaves join in the fun,
Tickling branches, everyone.
A hedgehog twirls, begins to spin,
He's just hoping not to win!

The sun peeks out with a grin,
As nature plays the tambourine.
Here in this place of whimsy bright,
Laughter echoes in pure delight!

Lush Retreat

Among the ferns, a party grew,
With tiny ants and one raccoon.
They played cards under a shady tree,
But lost the games to a bumblebee!

The mushrooms wore their little hats,
Proudly standing like little brats.
Even cacti jumped in too,
With prickly arms—they planned a coup!

A rabbit brought a carrot cake,
But other critters thought it fake.
They took a bite, then all agreed,
It tasted just like rabbit feed!

The sky burst forth with cloud balloons,
As laughter danced with little tunes.
Oh, how these creatures find their glee,
In this lush land of jubilee!

Sanctuary of the Sylvan

In a haven where laughter rings,
Woodpeckers tap and robins sing.
A raccoon wore a fancy vest,
Claiming he could host the best!

Critters gathered, what a sight!
Dancing circles, day and night.
A pony lost its little shoe,
Now does the polka for a crew!

The rabbits told the worst of jokes,
That made the turtles laugh in strokes.
A flickering firefly joined the queue,
Teaching them all a jig or two!

Among the trees where fun collides,
Each creature shows their joyful strides.
With nature's joke and laughter loud,
All find joy beneath the cloud!

A Tapestry of Foliage

Leaves are giggling in shades of green,
In the forest's dance, a funny scene.
A hedgehog slipped on a citrus peel,
Rolled down a hill—what a squeal!

The vines were gossiping, surely spry,
While the squirrels shared their prize: a pie!
Their table made of twigs and bark,
Lit by fireflies—oh, what a spark!

A toad joined in with a silly song,
Claimed he's the best, but smelled quite wrong.
Yet everyone cheered him on with glee,
As he croaked loud, a jubilee!

Through lively greens and the wayward paths,
Nature's laughter in endless drafts.
What a tale of joy and fun,
In this place where all can run!

Dew-Kissed Dawn

In the early light, frogs sing out of tune,
While a squirrel performs a clumsy balloon.
Dew drops sparkle on leaves, like tiny jewels,
Nature's own circus, where each critter drools.

A snail with ambition, dreaming of a race,
Trips on a twig, oh, such an embarrassing place!
Butterflies giggle as they flit to and fro,
While a bee wears a hat, putting on quite the show.

Trees gossip loudly, their leaves shaking green,
About a raccoon who thinks he's quite lean.
The sun peeks through branches, a mischievous prank,
Shining on creatures who danced and then drank.

As daisies are laughing at grasshoppers' moves,
Crickets are raving, while the owl just grooves.
The world starts waking with a chuckle and cheer,
In the morning mischief, so bright and so clear.

Enchanted by Greenery

In a thicket of laughter, where mushrooms convene,
A hedgehog jokes loudly, a true stand-up scene.
Bumblebees buzz with their pop and their flair,
Joking 'bout pollen, with fluffy, fat hair.

Vines swing like dancers, so bold and so free,
Lamenting the wisdom of a stubborn old bee.
A turtle in shades thinks he's cooler than cool,
Slipping on dew, he's the village's fool.

Closet of shadows, where giggles abound,
Rabbits make pancakes, flipping straight off the ground.
While toads do the tango, without any shoes,
Fungi appear as critics with slight, funny blues.

A toad's grand announcement: "I'm the king of this place!"
A ladybug whispers, "You've got flour on your face!"
The tease of the ferns tickles all who are near,
In this riot of green, laughter's all we hear.

Mingle of Moss and Moonlight

The moon tries to whisper with twinkling delight,
But a raccoon's too busy to notice the night.
With shiny black mask, he plots a small scheme,
While fireflies giggle, lighting up every dream.

Moss cushions the laughter, soft as a hug,
As owl tells tall tales of a wild woodland bug.
Frogs start a band with a showdown of croaks,
While hedges clap hands, cheering all of the jokes.

Crickets compete in a serenade show,
Where each one's a star and they all want to glow.
The starlit stage twinkles, no one is shy,
What a ridiculous mix, oh the fun we can spy!

Glowing glimmers cast spells, both funny and bright,
As night creatures gather in a whimsical flight.
With the rules of the game all governed by cheer,
In a cozy green nook, we conquer our fear.

Fern Fronds and Fables

Under fern fronds, a tale is retold,
Of a crow who loved glitter more than pure gold.
He strutted around with his sparkly pride,
While the sparrows just laughed and refused to abide.

A hedgehog with glasses, the librarian sage,
Tells stories of critters who've filled every page.
With thorns in his shoes, he wobbles with care,
Chasing squirrels that giggle, thinking life's quite fair.

As dew drips like honey on mushrooms so round,
The ants choreograph marathons on wet ground.
Worms negotiate rights for silkier beds,
While the gopher's still dreaming of wearing his threads.

The fables are silly, but the laughter is grand,
As creatures unite, each lending a hand.
In this whimsical world, where the weird takes flight,
The best kind of stories take shape in the night.

Moss-Covered Memories

In the woods where mushrooms laugh,
Old squirrels play their silly gaff.
Frogs croak tunes, a comedy show,
While ants march by in a line, oh no!

A robin's dance brings giggles near,
With wobbly steps, it spreads good cheer.
Bumblebees buzz, thinking they're grand,
But often crash into twigs that stand!

A raccoon in shades struts down the lane,
With swagger and pizzazz, what a silly name!
Dancing with shadows, trying out moves,
Oh, how nature's whimsy often grooves!

Pines lean in to share their jokes,
Tickling the air like mischievous folks.
In this snug nook, we laugh and run,
For laughter and pluck, it's all just fun!

A Symphony of Leaves

Whispers of wind tickle our ears,
As leaves giggle loud, dispelling fears.
An orchestra plays, with branches so spry,
With chirps and trills in the blue sky.

A waltz of willows sways with grace,
While squirrels compete for floor space.
With acorn hats and nuts in paws,
Their frolics draw laughter from all of us.

Crowd favorites: the chipmunks' spree,
Running in circles, oh so carefree!
While grasshoppers leap with a funny flair,
Two-step hopping, soaring through the air!

Beetles join in, a marching band,
With tiny drums, they create their stand.
As the sun dips low, we clap and sway,
To nature's beat, we laugh and play!

Beneath the Ancient Boughs

Under the trees where shadows shout,
The critters gather round, no doubt.
A wise old owl, with glasses perched,
Whispers the jokes nobody searched.

Squirrels argue over acorn bets,
While turtles debate on who gets upset.
A merry raccoon juggles pine cones,
Shattering silence with echoing tones.

Frogs don togas, a silly display,
Hosting a feast for their friends each day.
With flies for appetizers on big leaves,
"Bon appétit!" a lilypad heaves!

Laughter erupts as shadows high jinks,
As branches sway, they share their links.
In this haven where whims ignite,
We gather joy from morning to night!

Echoes of the Woodland

In a realm where echoes play,
Nature sings in a funny way.
Crouching weasels, stars of the show,
Tell tales of trees and twinkling glow.

In the brush, a dance unfolds,
With snickering seeds and stories told.
A bold little mouse leads a conga line,
While birds chirp rhymes, their voices entwined.

Beneath a mushroom, a party brews,
With ants serving snacks of morning dew.
As wind plays jokes, we giggle and sigh,
With nature's humor fluttering by.

Leaves clap hands in a raucous cheer,
As laughter spreads from ear to ear.
In this whimsical thicket, we're never alone,
For humor in nature feels like home!

Resplendent Refuge of Nature

In a jungle gym of vines, they swing,
Monkeys in shorts, what a sight to bring!
Parrots squawk jokes and giggle, oh dear,
Next to squirrels in spectacles sipping their beer.

Toads host a ball on lily pads bright,
Waltzing in moonlight, what a funny sight!
They croak 'We're all stars in the pond's grand show!'
While fish toss popcorn and cheer from below.

Mice tell tales of cheese that once flew,
While owls scratch their heads, convinced it's all true.
Trees giggle softly, their branches all sway,
As laughter cascades through the vibrant ballet.

In this lively land where the sillies convene,
The planet's a circus, a colorful scene!
Join the frolicsome friends in the sun,
For nature's a party, come on, let's run!

Emerald Oasis

In the shade of ferns, a picnic unfolds,
With ants in tuxedos, oh, how time holds!
They dance with the crumbs as if on a spree,
Declaring, "We're hungry! Bring snacks, look, whee!"

Frogs play leapfrog, a comical race,
As turtles slow clap, wearing smiles on their face.
A rabbit with glasses reads out loud,
While grasshoppers chirp, forming a crowd.

A parrot with style, a flamboyant chap,
Tells tales of a cat who once wore a map.
He squawks at the clouds as they giggle and tease,
While butterflies flutter, swaying with ease.

The breeze carries laughter, so light and so free,
In this wondrous haven, just come and see!
A joy-filled escape, nature's twist and turn,
With humor and fun, there's always more to learn!

Whispers of the Verdant

Under the boughs, where the shadows convene,
Gnomes play charades, what a quirky scene!
With shovels for props, they act out their tales,
While mushrooms giggle, their laughter prevails.

A skunk in a tutu enters with flair,
Dancing so boldly, no shame, take a dare!
The fireflies twinkle, they form a disco,
While crickets play beat on a leaf, what a show!

Beetles in bowties toast to a night,
Sipping on dew, their eyes wide with light.
"Here's to the nights that we borrow from dreams,
May we always be funny and bursting at seams!"

Whimsical whispers ride on the breeze,
Wrapping the night in such joyous unease.
In this land of laughter beneath the tree shade,
Nature throws parties, let's join, unafraid!

Solace in Leafy Shadows

In a patch of green, where giggles abound,
A hedgehog named Bertie rolls 'round and 'round.
He's dived into leaves, all big and all small,
With thorns all a-flutter, he's having a ball!

Squirrels debate, "Who can jump the most high?"
While raccoons in scarves exchange some sly pie.
They feast on the laughter and dance under stars,
Making a ruckus like rock stars with guitars!

A bear in a beret steals honey right slow,
But bees wear top hats and dance to and fro.
"Join us for tea!" they buzz with delight,
"We're sweetening up the most brilliant of nights!"

In shadows and laughter, this place sings and sways,
With whiskers and giggles, let's lighten our days.
A home filled with smiles, so vivid, so bright,
With humor enshrined, come bask in the light!

Reflections by the Stream

A fish in a hat thinks he's grand,
He's the best in all this wet land.
He wiggles and giggles with flair,
But really, he just loves the stare.

Frogs croak their tunes with delight,
In a chorus that sparks quite a fright.
They jump on a log, for a show,
And land with a plop, splash, and glow!

Sunshine bounces off water clear,
As turtles play cards without fear.
They bluff and they grumble, so sly,
"Draw a new shell? Oh, that's our try!"

A breeze tickles reeds, making them sway,
In this comical, nature-made ballet.
Where giggles float free, and the stream sings along,
Everything here feels like one funny song.

Meadow Songs

In a field where the daisies dance wild,
A grasshopper plays like a mischievous child.
He strums on a stalk with a tune all his own,
While butterflies giggle, in colors they've grown.

A snail with a suitcase dreams of the sea,
He's off to a vacation, he says, "Just wait for me!"
Though slow as molasses, he plans a grand trip,
On a leaf boat he'll sail, with a zippy snail zip!

The sun beams down, it's a party for ants,
They dance in a line, practicing their chants.
But one gets a wiggle in his tiny feet,
And tumbles right over—a most epic defeat!

The meadow's alive with its whimsical hums,
Where each quirky creature happily strums.
Their laughter rings out in a sweet, gentle breeze,
Nature's own concert, that aims to please.

Boughs of Solitude

An owl with a monocle thinks he's quite wise,
Perched high on a limb, under bright, starry skies.
He hoots out advice—with an air of chic fame,
Yet only the crickets know how he got that name.

A squirrel in pajamas sips nuts from a mug,
As night wraps the woods in its cozy, warm hug.
He chats with the shadows, sharing wild dreams,
Of acorns as treasures, or so it seems!

The branches all whisper their secrets aloud,
To the moonbeams that wrap them in silver-clad shroud.
And the fireflies flicker, in a witty debate,
On whether to glow, or to bicker, or wait!

In solitude there's fun, with friends all around,
Each tale and each laugh makes this place famed and sound.
These boughs hold a treasure—a lighthearted space,
Where nature's own comedy finds its own grace.

The Color of Calm

A penguin in shades, looking cool as can be,
Slides down a hill, giggling wildly with glee.
He's off to the beach—oh, what a grand sight!
But falls in a puddle, to his pure delight!

A llama with flair, wearing shoes that don't match,
Struts through the day, like he's ready to catch.
He causes a ruckus, as he prances about,
And all of the birds join in, flapping about!

The clouds wear a grin, floating high overhead,
With cotton-candy shapes, like a sweet dream instead.
And rainbows all giggle, forming links in the sky,
As colors conspire, making sure they fly high!

In this calm of laughter, with hues all aglow,
Life's little quirks dance like a shimmering show.
From quirky two-steppers to calm, gentle charms,
It's a joyful parade, where the heart softly warms.

Whispers of the Wildflower

In fields of bright and silly blooms,
The bees dance high, like tiny looms.
They whisper jokes in flowery tones,
While squirrels chuckle on mossy stones.

A hedgehog juggles acorns with flair,
As butterflies twirl in the warm spring air.
Each petal's a giggle, a secret delight,
In this patch of green, all feels just right.

Under a bumblebee's buzzing report,
The daisies play games at their floral sport.
A ladybug prances, her polka dots bold,
Telling stories of mischief, never old.

With worms as the spectators, the snails cheer loud,
In the vibrant garden, I'm always proud.
So join the laughter, let your heart fly,
In this wildflower realm, we shimmer and sigh.

Secluded in the Sunlight

Where sunbeams tickle the leaves of the trees,
The chipmunks giggle, 'Do you feel that breeze?'
A rabbit plays hide and seek with a stray,
While butterflies dance, in the warm light of day.

The ants throw a party, they've found some lost crumbs,
As the frogs croak their tunes, strumming tiny drums.
A squirrel in shades, he captures the scene,
Basking so boldly, he's quite the machine.

In this patch of warmth, laughter is free,
All critters join in, it's a jubilee!
A party of nature, all colors and cheer,
We dance and we sing, with nothing to fear.

The sun tickles noses, and smiles abound,
In this secret spot, joy can be found.
Hide in the warmth, let your heart swell,
In sunlight's embrace, all is just swell.

Kaleidoscope of Green

In a forest of giggles, plants wear their best,
The ferns tease the trees, who'd win in a jest?
Lush vines tell stories of laughter and play,
As colors collide in a dazzling display.

With greens that could tickle, and shades full of cheer,
A hedgehog cracks jokes that you just have to hear.
Moss carpets the ground, so soft and so bright,
Creating green cushions for naps in the light.

The flowers, they blend in a whimsical swirl,
Each petal a giggle, each stem a small twirl.
With dragonflies zipping, it's a race on the run,
'Try to catch me,' they whisper, 'Let's have some fun!'

A snail takes his time, says, 'I'll win this race,'
While worms do the worm in a muddy embrace.
In this riot of colors, we jump and we cheer,
In the kaleidoscope green, we forget all our fear.

Hushed by Nature's Breath

In a world where trees just love to confide,
The critters all gather, with giggles they bide.
Over giggly branches, the whispers do lie,
While grasshoppers chirp and the owls wink an eye.

The breeze plays the flute, with a hum and a sigh,
As squirrels in bow ties bring laughter nearby.
'Is it too much to ask for a dance in the shade?'
While blossoms throw petals, like confetti they made.

Nearby, a blue jay shows off his new beak,
With a feathered fan, saying, 'I'm chic not weak!'
The daisies reply with a flutter and bow,
'Join our parade, take a look at us now!'

As fawns leap and twirl, in a game of tag,
Even the shadows can't help but to wag.
In this whispered enclave, laughter floats wide,
Hushed by nature's breath, we stroll side by side.

Radiance of Nature's Heart

In the garden, a squirrel tries to dance,
But trips on a root, oh what a chance!
He shakes it off with flair and style,
Wonders if he's been outdone by a pile.

Bees buzzing round like they own the place,
Chasing their tails, they set quite the pace.
A flower yawns and says, "Not today!"
As honey and pollen have their silly play.

The sun peeks in, a mischievous tease,
Kissing the trees with a light, gentle breeze.
Laughing leaves whisper, "Is that all you got?"
"Let's play hide and seek, give it a shot!"

As the sky blushes in twilight's embrace,
Nature's antics bring smiles to our face.
Through laughter and joy, life's sweetened art,
Frolic and fun—it's nature's heart!

The Quiet Retreat

In a nook where the wildflowers bloom,
A rabbit thinks he has found a room.
He hops in circles, thinking it's grand,
But bumps his nose—oh, wasn't that planned?

A turtle ambles, slow and steady,
While squirrels pass by, feeling quite heady.
"Catch me if you can!" they tease and prance,
But tumble and roll—what a silly dance!

A frog croaks loudly, the king of the bog,
Swatting mosquitoes, he's quite the cog.
He inputs his croaks in rhythmic delight,
Hoping to make it to karaoke night!

When evening sets in with stars all aglow,
The nature show starts, a comedy flow.
With giggles and snores, the critters take part,
In this quiet retreat, we dance from the heart!

Verdure at Dusk

The meadow whispers, "Come take a peek!"
Where grasshoppers chatter with voices so chic.
They stage a debate by the old oak tree,
On who has the best hops—oh, what a spree!

A wise old owl gives a wink and a nod,
Watching the chaos, he feels quite odd.
"Do they ever tire? They bounce and they leap,"
While under his breath, he's catching some sleep.

Fireflies twinkle, like stars that fell low,
As night gives a wink, putting on quite the show.
"Oh look," says a rabbit, "a disco of light!"
"Let's dance through the meadows, till morning is bright!"

As dusk embraces, laughter fills the air,
Chasing away worries without any care.
This verdant escape is where mischief starts,
A playful reminder—nature has hearts!

Essence of Earth's Palette

In every corner, colors collide,
With splashes of joy that can't be denied.
Bluebirds are painting the sky with their song,
While daisies giggle, saying, "Join along!"

The pond reflects all the hues that we see,
As frogs turn to artists in their jubilee.
They dip in the water, splashing about,
Creating a masterpiece, there isn't a doubt!

But watch for the chameleon's shifty delight,
Changing his colors, he's ready for flight.
He grins as he blends with the grass by the rock,
Sipping on moonlight like it's a sweet shock!

As the palette unfolds in a quirky display,
Nature's humor tickles, in every way.
With laughter and color, life takes its stance,
In this essence of earth, let's all join the dance!

www.ingramcontent.com/pod-product-compliance
Lightning Source LLC
Chambersburg PA
CBHW050307120526
44590CB00016B/2526